Toys and

Contents

2		**Soft Toys**
4		**Toys with Wheels**
6		**Toys That Float**
8		**Building Toys**
10		**Ball Games**

Soft Toys

Some toys are soft. Teddy bears and dolls are soft.

You can hug them because they are soft.

Toys with Wheels

Some toys have wheels. Cars and trucks have wheels. So do trains.

You can push a car because it has wheels.

Toys That Float

Some toys float.
Boats and rubber ducks can float.

6

You can play with them in water because they float.

Building Toys

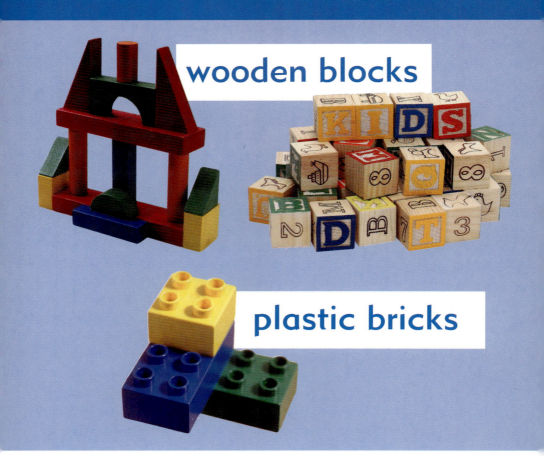

wooden blocks

plastic bricks

Some toys stack or fit together. Blocks stack. Bricks fit together.

You can build things with blocks and bricks.

Ball Games

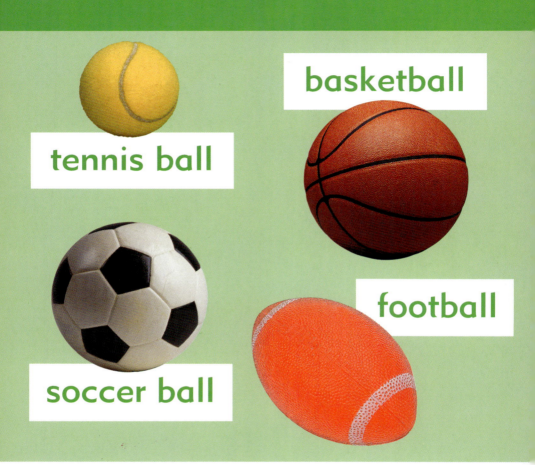

Ball games are fun to play. You can throw and catch a ball.

You can play ball games with your friends.

Which toys float?

12